Conten

University of Chester CAMPUS

Foreword	3
About this booklet	5

About religious education in the curriculum — 8

The contribution of religious education to the school curriculum	8
The structure of the national framework for religious education	10
Attitudes in religious education	13
Learning across the curriculum: the contribution of religious education	14
Religious education and the general teaching requirements	17

The non-statutory national framework for religious education — 19

Foundation stage	21
Key stage 1	24
Key stage 2	26
Key stage 3	28
Ages 14–19	30

The attainment targets for religious education — 33

Appendix: General teaching requirements — 38

Foreword

Every pupil in a maintained school has a statutory entitlement to religious education. This non-statutory national framework has been produced to support those with responsibility for the provision and quality of religious education in maintained schools. It lies at the heart of our policies to raise standards in the learning and teaching of religious education. It sets attainment targets for learning. The framework therefore gives local education authorities, Standing Advisory Councils on Religious Education, relevant authorities with responsibility for schools with a religious character, teachers, pupils, parents, employers and their wider communities a clear and shared understanding of the knowledge and skills that young people will gain at school. It allows schools to meet the individual learning needs of pupils and develop a distinctive character and ethos, rooted in their local communities. It also provides a framework within which all partners in education can support young people on the road to further learning.

Getting the framework right presented difficult choices and balances. It had to be robust enough to define and defend the knowledge, skills and understanding that is the entitlement of every pupil. At the same time it had to be flexible enough to give religious education syllabus providers the scope and creativity to enhance teaching and learning in religious education.

The focus of the framework is to set out a system that places value on the ethos and morals that religious education can establish, independent of any faith, and to promote high levels of consistency in teaching and learning. It should also give teachers the freedom to find the best ways to inspire in their pupils a joy and commitment to learning that will last a lifetime.

An entitlement to religious education must be an entitlement for all pupils, regardless of their faith or belief. This framework makes clear the principles that schools should follow in the teaching of religious education, to ensure that all pupils have the chance to succeed, whatever their individual needs or the potential barriers to their learning may be.

Equality of opportunity is part of the broad set of common values and purposes that underpin the school curriculum and the work of schools. These also include a commitment to valuing ourselves, our families and other relationships, the wider groups to which we belong, the environment in which we live and the diversity in our society. Pupils need to understand, therefore, the role and significance of religion in the modern world and the important beliefs and values that shape it.

This is the first non-statutory national framework for religious education in England. It will bring together the ways in which all pupils are helped to develop a full understanding of their roles and responsibilities as citizens in a modern democracy. It will play an important role alongside other aspects of the curriculum and school life, in helping pupils to engage with challenging spiritual, moral and social questions that arise in their lives and in society.

Good-quality religious education can transform pupils' assessment of themselves and others, and their understanding of the wider position of the world in which we live. This framework has been produced for the national improvement of religious education. It is strongly commended for use as early as possible.

Charles Clarke
Secretary of State for Education and Skills

Ken Boston, AO
Chief Executive, QCA

About this booklet

This booklet contains a non-statutory national framework for religious education. It:

■ sets out non-statutory guidelines for religious education in England

■ provides information to help those with responsibility for the provision and quality of religious education throughout the whole of the maintained system of education.

The national framework has been written mainly for:

■ local education authorities (LEAs)

■ Agreed Syllabus Conferences (ASCs)

■ Standing Advisory Councils on Religious Education (SACREs).

The national framework is also intended to:

■ be of use to the relevant authorities with responsibility for schools with a religious character

■ inform religious and secular communities about the scope of religious education.

The national framework will also be of interest to:

■ teachers, parents and pupils

■ school governors, managers and leaders

■ further education providers

■ providers of teacher education and training

■ inspectors and advisers

■ resources developers

■ others interested in religious education.

The national framework is intended to benefit all pupils by helping to improve the quality of religious education across the country.

This framework and materials that support the teaching, learning and assessment of religious education are on the QCA website (www.qca.org.uk).

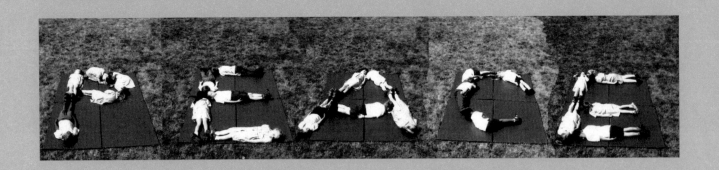

Religious education

I do like learning about RE because I like to know why other people believe in their God.

Hannah, age 9

RE . . . begins the process of you thinking . . . because it adds a deeper dimension to your life.

Surjit, age 14

RE tackles the most important questions in life and is therefore, for me, the most important school subject.

Jonathan, age 12

In my RE lessons I have learnt to become more broadminded, to accept other people's beliefs and faiths and to not let race or religion come in the way of what you see in an individual. What I like about my RE lessons is that my opinion is heard and I can find out what my fellow students' opinions are.

Francis, age 15

One important thing is to know and develop your way of thinking, and I think RE helps to do this. It also helps to teach respect, and to be true to others, and so also yourself. Also I think it is good, and even necessary, to have an open, educated mind, and it is interesting to learn about what other people – and very large groups of people – believe and why.

Keri, age 17

The importance of religious education

Religious education provokes challenging questions about the ultimate meaning and purpose of life, beliefs about God, the self and the nature of reality, issues of right and wrong and what it means to be human. It develops pupils' knowledge and understanding of Christianity, other principal religions, other religious traditions and other world views that offer answers to questions such as these. It offers opportunities for personal reflection and spiritual development. It enhances pupils' awareness and understanding of religions and beliefs, teachings, practices and forms of expression, as well as of the influence of religion on individuals, families, communities and cultures.

Religious education encourages pupils to learn from different religions, beliefs, values and traditions while exploring their own beliefs and questions of meaning. It challenges pupils to reflect on, consider, analyse, interpret and evaluate issues of truth, belief, faith and ethics and to communicate their responses.

Religious education encourages pupils to develop their sense of identity and belonging. It enables them to flourish individually within their communities and as citizens in a pluralistic society and global community. Religious education has an important role in preparing pupils for adult life, employment and lifelong learning. It enables pupils to develop respect for and sensitivity to others, in particular those whose faiths and beliefs are different from their own. It promotes discernment and enables pupils to combat prejudice.

I do not believe in God but I still enjoy RE. I like learning about other people's faiths.

Glenn, age 10

I think religion is the essence of a person's life so it's good to know about everyone's religion. I believe in my religion a lot and rely on it as a backbone to my life and depend on answers to my problems from it. So it interests me how other religions answer everyday problems and what views and reasons they have for their beliefs.

Farim, age 15

From RE lessons I have learnt about ethics and been given moral decisions to make. This taught me how to make choices and what is morally right and wrong. I have also been taught about many religions different to my own. This has given me an understanding of others' views and beliefs. I like discussing in RE because I like to hear other people's views.

Jessica, age 16

About religious education in the curriculum

The contribution of religious education to the school curriculum

Supporting the values of the curriculum

Religious education actively promotes the values of truth, justice, respect for all and care of the environment. It places specific emphasis on:

- pupils valuing themselves and others
- the role of family and the community in religious belief and activity
- the celebration of diversity in society through understanding similarities and differences
- sustainable development of the earth.

Religious education also recognises the changing nature of society, including changes in religious practice and expression, and the influence of religion in the local, national and global community.

Supporting the aims of the curriculum

Aim 1: The school curriculum should aim to provide opportunities for all pupils to learn and achieve.

Religious education should be a stimulating, interesting and enjoyable subject. The **Knowledge, skills and understanding** outlined in the national framework are designed to promote the best possible progress and attainment for all pupils. Religious education develops independent and interdependent learning. It makes an important contribution to pupils' skills in literacy and information and communication technology (ICT). Religious education promotes an enquiring approach in which pupils carefully consider issues of beliefs and truth in religion. It also enhances the capacity to think coherently and consistently. This enables pupils to evaluate thoughtfully their own and others' views in a reasoned and informed manner.

Aim 2: The school curriculum should aim to promote pupils' spiritual, moral, social and cultural development and prepare all pupils for the opportunities, responsibilities and experiences of life.

Religious education has a significant role in the promotion of spiritual, moral, social and cultural development (see page 14 for more guidance). At the heart of this national framework for religious education is a focus on ultimate questions and ethical issues. This focus enables pupils to appreciate their own and others' beliefs and cultures and how these impact on individuals, communities, societies and cultures. Religious education seeks to develop pupils' awareness of themselves and others. This helps pupils to gain a clear understanding of the significance of religions and beliefs in the world today and learn about the ways different faith communities relate to each other.

The national framework aims to promote religious understanding, discernment and respect and challenge prejudice and stereotyping. Religious education is committed to exploring the significance of the environment, both locally and globally, and the role of human beings and other species within it. A central concern of religious education is the promotion of each pupil's self-worth. A sense of self-worth helps pupils to reflect on their uniqueness as human beings, share their feelings and emotions with others and appreciate the importance of forming and maintaining positive relationships.

The purposes of the national framework

The national framework for religious education has four purposes, which mirror those of the National Curriculum.

1 **To establish an entitlement.** The national framework endorses an entitlement to learning in religious education for all pupils, irrespective of social background, culture, race, religion, gender, differences in ability and disabilities. This entitlement contributes to their developing knowledge, skills, understanding and attitudes. These are necessary for pupils' self-fulfilment and development as active and responsible citizens.

2 **To establish standards.** The national framework sets out expectations for learning and attainment that are explicit to pupils, parents, teachers, governors, employers and the public. It establishes standards for the performance of all pupils in religious education. These standards may be used to support assessment for learning. They may also be used to help pupils and teachers set targets for improvement and evaluate progress towards them.

3 **To promote continuity and coherence.** The national framework for religious education seeks to contribute to a coherent curriculum that promotes continuity. It helps the transition of pupils between schools and phases of education and can provide a foundation for further study and lifelong learning.

4 **To promote public understanding.** The national framework for religious education aims to increase public understanding of, and confidence in, the work of schools in religious education. It recognises the large extent to which the public is already involved with religious education, in the form of ASCs, SACREs, LEAs, governing bodies and the relevant religious and secular authorities and communities. It encourages those who are interested to participate in enriching the provision of religious education.

The structure of the national framework for religious education

The legal position

Religious education must be taught to all registered pupils in maintained schools,[1] including those in the sixth form, except to those withdrawn by their parents. This requirement does not apply to nursery classes in maintained schools.

Religious education is a component of the basic curriculum, to be taught alongside the National Curriculum in all maintained schools. In all maintained schools, other than voluntary aided schools with a religious character, it must be taught according to a locally agreed syllabus.[2]

Each LEA must convene an ASC to produce a syllabus. Once adopted by the LEA, the programme of study of the agreed syllabus sets out what pupils should be taught. The attainment levels set out the expected standards of pupils' performance at different ages. The Education Act 1996 states that an agreed syllabus must reflect the fact that the religious traditions in Great Britain are in the main Christian, while taking account of the teachings and practices of the other principal religions represented in Great Britain. Each LEA must have a SACRE. The SACRE may require a review of the agreed syllabus at any time. This is in addition to the requirement on LEAs to convene a conference to reconsider the agreed syllabus every five years.

Using the national framework to inform syllabus development

The national framework sets out a structure for ASCs and faith communities to use to determine what pupils should be taught in religious education. The national framework has been designed to be inclusive, setting out guidance on the teaching and learning of religious education that is appropriate for all schools including faith schools. It is for each LEA, through its ASC, to determine the extent to which the national framework informs syllabus development. Similarly, the local, regional and national authorities within faith communities should consider what account they wish to take of the national framework.

The national framework

The national framework sets out what pupils should study in religious education from the ages of 3 to 19. It is organised in three sections for pupils of different ages:
- foundation stage
- key stages 1, 2 and 3
- ages 14–19.

These are followed by the attainment targets and level descriptions.

The National Curriculum general teaching requirements, which are a statutory requirement across National Curriculum subjects, are included as an appendix.

---

[1] The legal requirements for teaching religious education are set out in the Education Act 1996 and School Standards and Framework Act 1998. Parents have the right to withdraw their children from all or part of religious education lessons.

[2] See School Standards and Framework Act 1998 for variations on this requirement.

The foundation stage (ages 3–5)

Curriculum guidance for the foundation stage (QCA, 2000) sets out expectations of what pupils should learn to meet the early learning goals. The national framework describes how religious education can contribute to the early learning goals and provides examples of religious education-related activities.

Key stages 1, 2 and 3 (ages 5–14)

The national framework follows the same format as the National Curriculum programmes of study[3] with sections on knowledge, skills and understanding and breadth of study.

Knowledge, skills and understanding

The knowledge, skills and understanding identify the key aspects of learning in religious education. These are described as 'learning about religion' and 'learning from religion'.

Learning about religion includes enquiry into, and investigation of, the nature of religion, its beliefs, teachings and ways of life, sources, practices and forms of expression. It includes the skills of interpretation, analysis and explanation. Pupils learn to communicate their knowledge and understanding using specialist vocabulary. It also includes identifying and developing an understanding of ultimate questions[4] and ethical issues. In the national framework, learning about religion covers pupils' knowledge and understanding of individual religions and how they relate to each other as well as the study of the nature and characteristics of religion.

Learning from religion is concerned with developing pupils' reflection on and response to their own and others' experiences in the light of their learning about religion. It develops pupils' skills of application, interpretation and evaluation of what they learn about religion. Pupils learn to develop and communicate their own ideas, particularly in relation to questions of identity and belonging, meaning, purpose and truth, and values and commitments.

> In teaching religious education, it is vital that the skills are developed through the knowledge and understanding, and vice versa. It is also important that pupils understand how their learning in religious education is progressing, and what they need to do to improve it.

Breadth of study

The knowledge, skills and understanding are developed through the breadth of study,[5] which has three elements:

- religions and beliefs
- themes
- experiences and opportunities.

> When developing schemes of work, it is important to balance the three elements of the breadth of study. At times learning will focus on the discrete study of a religion. On other occasions, the theme or experience will be the central element. It is of course possible to combine all three elements. For example, visiting a place of worship can enhance the theme of symbols as well as develop knowledge and understanding of the religion being studied.

[3] The Education Act 2000 defines a programme of study as the 'matters, skills and processes' that should be taught to pupils of different abilities and maturities during the key stage.
[4] Ultimate questions refer to the study within religious education of questions such as 'Is God real?', 'Why are we alive?', 'What is meant by good and evil?', 'Why do people suffer?'. These are powerful questions about beliefs and values.
[5] The breadth of study is defined as the context, activities, areas of study and range of experiences that pupils encounter at the different key stages.

Religions and beliefs

The national framework affirms the legal basis of religious education and gives non-statutory guidance for ASCs and faith communities to consider in determining which religions are to be studied. It is important to make sure that the legal requirements for religious education are met and that the religious education curriculum is broad and balanced.

To make sure the requirements are met and the curriculum is broad and balanced:
- Christianity should be studied throughout each key stage
- the other principal religions represented in Great Britain (here regarded as Buddhism, Hinduism, Islam, Judaism and Sikhism) should be studied across the key stages. It is important that ASCs and schools ensure that by the end of key stage 3 pupils have encountered all of these five principal religions in sufficient depth.

It is also essential that religious education enables pupils to share their own beliefs, viewpoints and ideas without embarrassment or ridicule. Many pupils come from religious backgrounds but others have no attachment to religious beliefs and practices. To ensure that all pupils' voices are heard and the religious education curriculum is broad and balanced, it is recommended that there are opportunities for all pupils to study:
- other religious traditions such as the Bahá'í faith, Jainism and Zoroastrianism
- secular philosophies such as humanism.

Pupils should also study how religions relate to each other, recognising both similarities and differences within and between religions. They should be encouraged to reflect on:
- the significance of interfaith dialogue
- the important contribution religion can make to community cohesion and the combating of religious prejudice and discrimination.

Themes

The themes provide the context for 'learning about religion' and 'learning from religion'. They may be taught separately, in combination with other themes, or as part of religions and beliefs. However the themes are combined, the knowledge, skills and understanding should be covered with sufficient breadth and depth. The specificity of content, both in terms of religions and beliefs studied and themes, is the legal responsibility of the ASC or faith community.

Experiences and opportunities

Pupils should be provided with a range of experiences and opportunities that can enrich and broaden their learning in religious education.

Ages 14–19

This framework sets out an entitlement for all students to study religious education and to have their learning accredited.

Attitudes in religious education

While the knowledge, skills and understanding are central to the national framework for religious education, it is also vital that religious education encourages pupils to develop positive attitudes to their learning and to the beliefs and values of others. The following four attitudes are essential for good learning in religious education and should be developed at each stage or phase of religious education:

- self-awareness
- respect for all
- open-mindedness
- appreciation and wonder.

Self-awareness in religious education includes pupils:

- feeling confident about their own beliefs and identity and sharing them without fear of embarrassment or ridicule
- developing a realistic and positive sense of their own religious, moral and spiritual ideas
- recognising their own uniqueness as human beings and affirming their self-worth
- becoming increasingly sensitive to the impact of their ideas and behaviour on other people.

Respect for all in religious education includes pupils:

- developing skills of listening and a willingness to learn from others, even when others' views are different from their own
- being ready to value difference and diversity for the common good
- appreciating that some beliefs are not inclusive and considering the issues that this raises for individuals and society
- being prepared to recognise and acknowledge their own bias
- being sensitive to the feelings and ideas of others.

Open-mindedness in religious education includes pupils:

- being willing to learn and gain new understanding
- engaging in argument or disagreeing reasonably and respectfully (without belittling or abusing others) about religious, moral and spiritual questions
- being willing to go beyond surface impressions
- distinguishing between opinions, viewpoints and beliefs in connection with issues of conviction and faith.

Appreciation and wonder in religious education includes pupils:

- developing their imagination and curiosity
- recognising that knowledge is bounded by mystery
- appreciating the sense of wonder at the world in which they live
- developing their capacity to respond to questions of meaning and purpose.

At each key stage, the framework identifies examples of specific opportunities for developing these attitudes.

Greater emphasis on this aspect in faith schools

Learning across the curriculum: the contribution of religious education

The importance of religious education is set out on page 7. This section sets out in general terms how religious education can promote learning across the curriculum in a number of areas such as spiritual, moral, social and cultural development, key skills and thinking skills.

Promoting spiritual, moral, social and cultural development through religious education

Religious education provides opportunities to promote *spiritual development* through:

- discussing and reflecting on key questions of meaning and truth such as the origins of the universe, life after death, good and evil, beliefs about God and values such as justice, honesty and truth
- learning about and reflecting on important concepts, experiences and beliefs that are at the heart of religious and other traditions and practices
- considering how beliefs and concepts in religion may be expressed through the creative and expressive arts and related to the human and natural sciences, thereby contributing to personal and communal identity
- considering how religions and other world views perceive the value of human beings, and their relationships with one another, with the natural world, and with God
- valuing relationships and developing a sense of belonging
- developing their own views and ideas on religious and spiritual issues.

Religious education provides opportunities to promote *moral development* through:

- enhancing the values identified within the National Curriculum, particularly valuing diversity and engaging in issues of truth, justice and trust
- exploring the influence of family, friends and media on moral choices and how society is influenced by beliefs, teachings, sacred texts and guidance from religious leaders
- considering what is of ultimate value to pupils and believers through studying the key beliefs and teachings from religion and philosophy about values and ethical codes of practice
- studying a range of ethical issues, including those that focus on justice, to promote racial and religious respect and personal integrity
- considering the importance of rights and responsibilities and developing a sense of conscience.

Religious education provides opportunities to promote *social development* through:

- considering how religious and other beliefs lead to particular actions and concerns
- investigating social issues from religious perspectives, recognising the diversity of viewpoints within and between religions as well as the common ground between religions
- articulating pupils' own and others' ideas on a range of contemporary social issues.

Religious education provides opportunities to promote *cultural development* through:

- encountering people, literature, the creative and expressive arts and resources from differing cultures
- considering the relationship between religion and cultures and how religions and beliefs contribute to cultural identity and practices
- promoting racial and interfaith harmony and respect for all, combating prejudice and discrimination, contributing positively to community cohesion and promoting awareness of how interfaith cooperation can support the pursuit of the common good.

Promoting citizenship through religious education

Religious education plays a significant part in promoting *citizenship* through:

- developing pupils' knowledge and understanding about the diversity of national, regional, religious and ethnic identities in the United Kingdom and the need for mutual respect and understanding
- enabling pupils to think about topical spiritual, moral, social and cultural issues including the importance of resolving conflict fairly
- exploring the rights, responsibilities and duties of citizens locally, nationally and globally
- enabling pupils to justify and defend orally, and in writing, personal opinions about issues, problems and events.

Promoting personal, social and health education through religious education

Religious education plays a significant part in promoting *personal, social and health education* through pupils:

- developing confidence and responsibility and making the most of their abilities by learning about what is fair and unfair, right and wrong and being encouraged to share their opinions
- developing a healthy, safer lifestyle by learning about religious beliefs and teachings on drug use and misuse, food and drink, leisure, relationships and human sexuality, learning about the purpose and value of religious beliefs and sensitivities in relation to sex education and enabling pupils to consider and express their own views
- developing good relationships and respecting the differences between people by learning about the diversity of different ethnic and religious groups and the destructive power of prejudice, challenging racism, discrimination, offending behaviour and bullying, being able to talk about relationships and feelings, considering issues of marriage and family life and meeting and encountering people whose beliefs, views and lifestyles are different from their own.

Promoting key skills through religious education

Religious education provides opportunities for pupils to develop the key skills of:

- *communication* through developing a broad and accurate religious vocabulary, reading and responding to a range of written and spoken language (including sacred texts, stories, poetry, prayers, liturgy and worship), communicating ideas using the creative and expressive arts, talking and writing with understanding and insight about religious and other beliefs and values, reflecting critically on ultimate questions of life, using reasoned arguments

- *application of number* through calendrical reckoning, collecting, recording, presenting and interpreting data involving graphs, charts and statistical analysis
- *information technology* through using CD-ROMs and the internet selectively, researching information about religions and beliefs, teaching and practices, using email to communicate and analyse information with people of differing beliefs and cultures, using spreadsheets and databases to handle and present data relevant to the study of religious education
- *working with others* through sharing ideas, discussing beliefs, values and practices, collaborating with each other and developing respect and sensitivity
- *improving own learning and performance* through setting targets as part of religious education development, reviewing their achievements and identifying ways to improve their own work
- *problem solving* through recognising key issues to do with religious belief, practice and expression, interpreting and explaining findings and making personal decisions on religious issues (for example, considering their own and religious ideas on good and evil), ethical dilemmas and priorities in life.

Promoting other aspects of the curriculum

Religious education provides opportunities to promote:

- *thinking skills* through helping pupils to research, select, interpret and analyse information from religious traditions, reflect and question their own views and ideas and those of others and communicate their ideas in a variety of ways
- *financial capability* through considering the responsible use of money, the importance of giving and the ethics of wealth, debt, poverty, gambling, business and investment
- *creativity and culture* through considering the scope of human nature, sources of inspiration and discovery, connections between beliefs, values and forms of artistic expression, appreciating the value of cultural distinctiveness and reflecting on beauty, goodness and truth in creative and expressive arts
- *education for racial equality and community cohesion* through studying the damaging effects of xenophobia and racial stereotyping, the impact of conflict in religion and the promotion of respect, understanding and cooperation through dialogue between people of different faiths and beliefs
- *effective contributions to scientific, medical and health issues* through exploring philosophical and ethical questions of the origin, purpose and destiny of the cosmos and life within it, exploring the nature of humanity and human interaction with the world, exploring developments in genetics and medicine and their application and use and exploring concepts of health and well-being and their promotion
- *links to employment, vocations and work-related learning* through a focus on individual sense of purpose and aspiration in life, and through considering the appropriateness and relevance of religious education to a wide range of employment opportunities and the development of spiritual and ethical issues linked to the world of work
- *education for sustainable development* through helping pupils consider the origins and value of life, the importance of looking after the environment and studying the ways in which religious beliefs and teachings have influenced attitudes to the environment and other species.

Religious education and the general teaching requirements

This section outlines the particular contribution religious education can make to the general teaching requirements of the National Curriculum. These are included as an appendix.

Religious education and inclusion

Religious education can make a significant contribution to inclusion, particularly in its focus on promoting respect for all. The national framework for religious education contains many references to the role of religious education in challenging stereotypical views and appreciating, positively, differences in others. The national framework enables all pupils to consider the impact of people's beliefs on their own actions and lifestyle. The national framework also highlights the importance of religions and beliefs and how religious education can develop pupils' self-esteem.

Effective inclusion involves teaching a lively, stimulating religious education curriculum that:

- builds on and is enriched by the differing experiences pupils bring to religious education
- meets all pupils' learning needs including those with learning difficulties or who are gifted and talented, boys and girls, pupils for whom English is an additional language, pupils from all religious communities and pupils from a wide range of ethnic groups and diverse family backgrounds.

To overcome any potential barriers to learning in religious education, some pupils may require:

- support to access text, such as through prepared tapes, particularly when working with significant quantities of written materials or at speed
- help to communicate their ideas through methods other than extended writing, where this is a requirement. For example, pupils may demonstrate their understanding through speech or the use of ICT
- a non-visual way of accessing sources of information when undertaking research in aspects of religious education, for example using audio materials.

Religious education and the use of language

Religious education can make an important contribution to pupils' use of language
by enabling them to:

- acquire and develop a specialist vocabulary
- communicate their ideas with depth and precision
- listen to the views and ideas of others, including people from religious traditions
- be enthused about the power and beauty of language, recognising its limitations
- develop their speaking and listening skills when considering religions, beliefs and
  ideas and articulating their responses
- read, particularly from sacred texts
- write in different styles, such as poetry, diaries, extended writing and the
  synthesis of differing views, beliefs and ideas
- evaluate clearly and rationally, using a range of reasoned, balanced arguments.

Religious education and the use of information and communication technology

Religious education can make an important contribution to pupils' use of ICT by
enabling pupils to:

- make appropriate use of the internet or CD-ROM sources to investigate, analyse
  and evaluate different aspects of religious beliefs and practices, ultimate
  questions and ethical issues
- use email or videoconferencing to communicate and collaborate with individuals
  in different locations, enabling associations to be made between religions and
  individual, national and international life
- use multimedia and presentation software to communicate a personal response,
  the essence of an argument or a stimulus for discussion
- use writing-support and concept-mapping software to organise thoughts and
  communicate knowledge and understanding of the diversity of belief and
  practice within and between religious traditions
- use equipment such as digital cameras and digital video to bring authentic
  images into the classroom to support discussion and reflection, and to enhance
  understanding of the impact of religious beliefs and practices on the lives of
  local individuals and faith communities.

The non-statutory national framework for religious education

The non-statutory national framework: religious education

Foundation stage

The foundation stage describes the phase of a child's education from the age of 3 to the end of reception at the age of 5. Religious education is statutory for all pupils registered on the school roll. The statutory requirement for religious education does not extend to nursery classes in maintained schools and is not, therefore, a legal requirement for much of the foundation stage. It may, however, form a valuable part of the educational experience of children throughout the key stage.

The contribution of religious education to the early learning goals

The early learning goals set out what most children should achieve by the end of the foundation stage. The six areas of learning identified in these goals are:

- personal, social and emotional development
- communication, language and literacy
- mathematical development
- knowledge and understanding of the world
- physical development
- creative development.

Religious education can make an active contribution to all these areas but has a particularly important contribution to make to:

- personal, social and emotional development
- communication, language and literacy
- knowledge and understanding of the world
- creative development.

For each of these four areas, there are examples of religious education-related experiences and opportunities and an activity. Each activity is indicative only and is included to exemplify particular ways in which religious education-related activities contribute to the early learning goals.

During the foundation stage, children may begin to explore the world of religion in terms of special people, books, times, places and objects and by visiting places of worship. They listen to and talk about stories. They may be introduced to religious words and use their senses in exploring religions and beliefs, practices and forms of expression. They reflect on their own feelings and experiences. They use their imagination and curiosity to develop their appreciation and wonder of the world in which they live.

Early learning goals

Self-confidence and self-esteem
- respond to significant experiences showing a range of feelings when appropriate
- have a developing awareness of their own needs, views and feelings and be sensitive to the needs, views and feelings of others
- have a developing respect for their own cultures and beliefs and those of other people.

Making relationships
- work as part of group or class, taking turns, sharing fairly, understanding that there need to be agreed values and codes of behaviour for groups of people including adults and children, to work together harmoniously.

Behaviour and self-control
- understand what is right, what is wrong and why
- consider the consequences of their words and actions for themselves and others.

Sense of community
- understand that people have different needs, views, cultures and beliefs that need to be treated with respect
- understand that they can expect others to treat their needs, views, cultures and beliefs with respect.

Language for communication
- listen with enjoyment and respond to stories, songs and other music, rhymes and poems and make up their own stories, songs, rhymes and poems
- extend their vocabulary, exploring the meaning and sounds of new words.

Language for thinking
- use language to imagine and recreate roles and experiences
- use talk to organise, sequence and clarify thinking, ideas, feelings and events.

Reading
- retell narratives in the correct sequence, drawing on language patterns of stories.

Personal, social and emotional development

Examples of religious education-related experiences and opportunities
- Children use some stories from religious traditions as a stimulus to reflect on their own feelings and experiences and explore them in various ways.
- Using a story as a stimulus, children reflect on the words and actions of characters and decide what they would have done in a similar situation. They learn about the story and its meanings through activity and play.
- Using role-play as a stimulus, children talk about some of the ways that people show love and concern for others and why this is important.
- Children think about issues of right and wrong and how humans help one another.

Example of an activity

In the context of a learning theme to do with 'growing' or 'the natural world', children encounter the parable of the mustard seed. They look at and talk about some tiny seeds and the teacher tells the parable, putting it into context as a story Jesus told. The teacher emphasises how, in the story, the tree that grew from the little seed became a safe home for birds. Children talk about what helps them to feel safe. They take a walk to look at trees and touch trees. They think about how they should look after trees. They talk about what it would be like to fly up into the branches. They plant seeds and role-play the growth of the seed in dance. They produce shared or independent writing on what they would like to grow into. Through these experiences children become more aware of themselves, for example of the concepts 'I am growing' 'I need to feel safe'. They respond to the significant experiences of exploring a story and wonder at the growth of seeds. They learn to understand their responsibility to the natural world and begin to consider beliefs about Jesus.

Communication, language and literacy

Examples of religious education-related experiences and opportunities
- Children have opportunities to respond creatively, imaginatively and meaningfully to memorable experiences.
- Using a religious celebration as a stimulus, children talk about the special events associated with the celebration.
- Through artefacts, stories and music, children learn about important religious celebrations.

Example of an activity

In the context of a learning theme to do with 'books' or 'favourite stories', children look at a child's Haggadah and are encouraged to ask questions about it. The children are told that the book belongs to a Jewish child who is celebrating Passover. The story of Passover is briefly told. Children are invited to think about their favourite books. The teacher talks about the child learning Hebrew and having an important job to do at the celebration meal. Children think about where and how they learn and how it feels to do something really well. They learn the words 'Jewish' and 'Hebrew'. They use language in role-playing a family meal. They look at and talk about a variety of dual-language books, share other old stories from both oral and written traditions and make a class book based on a favourite story or a celebration they have shared. A questions board is set up for children to record any questions that come into their heads. Through these experiences, they learn about the importance of story and sacred texts in religion, develop respect for the beliefs and values of others and extend their vocabulary.

Knowledge and understanding of the world

Examples of religious education-related experiences and opportunities

- Children ask and answer questions about religion and culture, as they occur naturally within their everyday experiences.
- Children visit places of worship.
- They listen to and respond to a wide range of religious and ethnic groups.
- They handle artefacts with curiosity and respect.
- Having visited a local place of worship, children learn new words associated with the place, showing respect.

Example of an activity

In the context of a learning theme to do with 'buildings' or 'special places', children are shown a selection of pictures. They then learn about three different places children go with their families to worship God: a church, the Golden Temple and a mosque. Children are invited to talk about the pictures of places of worship, looking for common and distinctive features. Children talk about somewhere they have been that they will remember. They go out and photograph significant places (and people) in the local area and display their pictures in school. They visit a place of worship and record what they see. They talk about building materials and how they are used. They look at patterns. They sort collections of photographs of buildings and they compare buildings in their local environment and far away, talking particularly about the local church, the Golden Temple and the mosque. Through these experiences, children learn about the importance of places of worship, relating this to their own special places. They begin to be aware of their own cultures and beliefs and those of other people.

Creative development

Examples of religious education-related experiences and opportunities

- Using religious artefacts as a stimulus, children think about and express meanings associated with the artefact.
- Children share their own experiences and feelings and those of others, and are supported in reflecting on them.

Example of an activity

In the context of a learning theme to do with 'water', 'journeys' or 'the natural world', children look at a sealed pot that has water from the Ganges river inside it. Once they know that the pot contains water, they are encouraged to imagine a wide, flowing river. They look at photographs or videos of rivers and waterfalls and talk about how water moves. They hear the story of the birth of the river Ganges (regarded by Hindus as sacred). The teacher emphasises that it is a story that helps some people imagine what God might be like. They look at photographs of Hindus bathing in the Ganges and talk about why the river is important to them. They are invited to think about their ideas about heaven. In response to the story, they explore water through play. They create a great river collage, using a variety of media. They make a river dance, using lengths of coloured fabric and accompany it with percussion music. Through these experiences, children develop their imagination through a variety of creative and expressive arts. They begin to think about the importance of water as a symbol in religion and why some people regard particular places as sacred.

Early learning goals

Exploration and investigation
- investigate objects and materials by using all of their senses as appropriate
- find out about and identify some features of living things, objects and events they observe.

Information and communication technology
- use information and communication technology to support their learning.

A sense of time
- find out about past and present events in their own lives, and in those of their families and other people they know.

A sense of place
- find out about their environment and talk about those features they like and dislike.

Cultures and beliefs
- begin to know about their own cultures and beliefs and those of other people.

Imagination
- use their imagination in art and design, music, dance, imaginative play, role-play and stories.

Responding to experiences, and expressing and communicating ideas
- respond in a variety of ways to what they see, hear, smell, touch and feel.

Throughout key stage 1, pupils explore Christianity and at least one other principal religion. They learn about different beliefs about God and the world around them. They encounter and respond to a range of stories, artefacts and other religious materials. They learn to recognise that beliefs are expressed in a variety of ways, and begin to use specialist vocabulary. They begin to understand the importance and value of religion and belief, especially for other children and their families. Pupils ask relevant questions and develop a sense of wonder about the world, using their imaginations. They talk about what is important to them and others, valuing themselves, reflecting on their own feelings and experiences and developing a sense of belonging.

1a → Links to other subjects
This builds on En1/11b, where pupils in drama activities present stories to others and En1/2c–e, where pupils make relevant comments, listen to others' reactions and ask questions to clarify their understanding.

1a–b → ICT opportunity
Pupils could use the internet or CD-ROMs to obtain a wide range of stories about religious beliefs and teachings.

1c → Attitudes
Pupils have the opportunity to develop respect for all.

2a → Links to other subjects
This builds on Gg1c and 3a, where pupils express their own views about places and environments, which can lead to reflection on spiritual experiences and concepts.

2a → Attitudes
Pupils have the opportunity to develop appreciation and wonder.

2c–d → Links to other subjects
These build on PSHE/Ci1a–b, 2c and 2e, where pupils are taught about what is fair and unfair, right and wrong, to share their opinion on things that matter to them, to recognise choices they make and to realise that people and other living things have needs and they have responsibilities to meet them.

The non-statutory national framework: religious education

Key stage 1

Knowledge, skills and understanding

Learning about religion

1 Pupils should be taught to:
   a explore a range of religious stories and sacred writings and talk about their meanings
   b name and explore a range of celebrations, worship and rituals in religion, noting similarities where appropriate
   c identify the importance, for some people, of belonging to a religion and recognise the difference this makes to their lives
   d explore how religious beliefs and ideas can be expressed through the arts and communicate their responses
   e identify and suggest meanings for religious symbols and begin to use a range of religious words.

Learning from religion

2 Pupils should be taught to:
   a reflect on and consider religious and spiritual feelings, experiences and concepts such as worship, wonder, praise, thanks, concern, joy and sadness
   b ask and respond imaginatively to puzzling questions, communicating their ideas
   c identify what matters to them and others, including those with religious commitments, and communicate their responses
   d reflect on how spiritual and moral values relate to their own behaviour
   e recognise that religious teachings and ideas make a difference to individuals, families and the local community.

Breadth of study

3 During the key stage, pupils should be taught the **Knowledge, skills and understanding** through the following areas of study:

Religions and beliefs

a Christianity

b at least one other principal religion

c a religious community with a significant local presence, where appropriate

d a secular world view, where appropriate

Themes

e believing: what people believe about God, humanity and the natural world

f story: how and why some stories are sacred and important in religion

g celebrations: how and why celebrations are important in religion

h symbols: how and why symbols express religious meaning

i leaders and teachers: figures who have an influence on others locally, nationally and globally in religion

j belonging: where and how people belong and why belonging is important

k myself: who I am and my uniqueness as a person in a family and community

Experiences and opportunities

l visiting places of worship and focusing on symbols and feelings

m listening and responding to visitors from local faith communities

n using their senses and having times of quiet reflection

o using art and design, music, dance and drama to develop their creative talents and imagination

p sharing their own beliefs, ideas and values and talking about their feelings and experiences

q beginning to use ICT to explore religions and beliefs as practised in the local and wider community.

3i → Links to other subjects
This builds on Hi6c, where pupils are taught about the lives of significant men, women and children drawn from the history of Britain and the wider world.

3l → ICT opportunity
Pupils could use digital recording equipment to enhance their learning about places of worship.

3m → ICT opportunity
Pupils could record their work using digital video and use ICT painting, desktop publishing or multimedia authoring packages.

Throughout key stage 2, pupils learn about Christianity and at least two of the other principal religions, recognising the impact of religion and belief locally, nationally and globally. They make connections between differing aspects of religion and consider the different forms of religious expression. They consider the beliefs, teachings, practices and ways of life central to religion. They learn about sacred texts and other sources and consider their meanings. They begin to recognise diversity in religion, learning about similarities and differences both within and between religions and beliefs and the importance of dialogue between them. They extend the range and use of specialist vocabulary. They recognise the challenges involved in distinguishing between ideas of right and wrong, and valuing what is good and true. They communicate their ideas, recognising other people's viewpoints. They consider their own beliefs and values and those of others in the light of their learning in religious education.

1a–b → Links to other subjects
These build on PSHE/Ci4b, where pupils are taught about the lives of people in other places and times, and people with different values and customs.

1a–d → ICT opportunity
Pupils can use ICT to find information on a variety of subjects and use ICT tools to present their findings.

1b → Links to other subjects
This builds on Hi2b, where pupils learn about the social, cultural, religious and ethnic diversity of societies in Britain and the wider world.

1d → Attitudes
Pupils have the opportunity to develop open-mindedness.

1e → Links to other subjects
This requirement builds on Mu5e, where pupils develop their skills through a range of live and recorded music from different times and cultures.

1g → Links to other subjects
This requirement builds on En2 and 5a, where pupils are taught to identify the use and effect of specialist vocabulary.

The non-statutory national framework: religious education

Key stage 2

Knowledge, skills and understanding

Learning about religion

1 Pupils should be taught to:

a describe the key aspects of religions, especially the people, stories and traditions that influence the beliefs and values of others

b describe the variety of practices and ways of life in religions and understand how these stem from, and are closely connected with, beliefs and teachings

c identify and begin to describe the similarities and differences within and between religions

d investigate the significance of religion in the local, national and global communities

e consider the meaning of a range of forms of religious expression, understand why they are important in religion and note links between them

f describe and begin to understand religious and other responses to ultimate and ethical questions

g use specialist vocabulary in communicating their knowledge and understanding

h use and interpret information about religions from a range of sources.

Learning from religion

2 Pupils should be taught to:

a reflect on what it means to belong to a faith community, communicating their own and others' responses

b respond to the challenges of commitment both in their own lives and within religious traditions, recognising how commitment to a religion is shown in a variety of ways

c discuss their own and others' views of religious truth and belief, expressing their own ideas

d reflect on ideas of right and wrong and their own and others' responses to them

e reflect on sources of inspiration in their own and others' lives.

Breadth of study

3   During the key stage, pupils should be taught the **Knowledge, skills and understanding** through the following areas of study:

Religions and beliefs

a   Christianity

b   at least two other principal religions

c   a religious community with a significant local presence, where appropriate

d   a secular world view, where appropriate

Themes

e   beliefs and questions: how people's beliefs about God, the world and others impact on their lives

f   teachings and authority: what sacred texts and other sources say about God, the world and human life

g   worship, pilgrimage and sacred places: where, how and why people worship, including at particular sites

h   the journey of life and death: why some occasions are sacred to believers, and what people think about life after death

i   symbols and religious expression: how religious and spiritual ideas are expressed

j   inspirational people: figures from whom believers find inspiration

k   religion and the individual: what is expected of a person in following a religion or belief

l   religion, family and community: how religious families and communities practise their faith, and the contributions this makes to local life

m   beliefs in action in the world: how religions and beliefs respond to global issues of human rights, fairness, social justice and the importance of the environment

Experiences and opportunities

n   encountering religion through visitors and visits to places of worship, and focusing on the impact and reality of religion on the local and global community

o   discussing religious and philosophical questions, giving reasons for their own beliefs and those of others

p   considering a range of human experiences and feelings

q   reflecting on their own and others' insights into life and its origin, purpose and meaning

r   expressing and communicating their own and others' insights through art and design, music, dance, drama and ICT

s   developing the use of ICT, particularly in enhancing pupils' awareness of religions and beliefs globally.

2d → Attitudes
Pupils have the opportunity to develop self-awareness.

3e–m → ICT opportunity
Pupils could find information on the internet and CD-ROMs and could use email, particularly to share their views on global issues of human rights, social justice and the importance of the environment.

3l → Links to other subjects
This requirement builds on Gg6a–b, where pupils investigate a locality in the UK and a locality in a country that is less economically developed. They can consider the contribution of religion to local life.

The non-statutory national framework: religious education

Key stage 3

Knowledge, skills and understanding

Learning about religion

1 Pupils should be taught to:

   a investigate and explain the differing impacts of religious beliefs and teachings on individuals, communities and societies

   b analyse and explain how religious beliefs and ideas are transmitted by people, texts and traditions

   c investigate and explain why people belong to faith communities and explain the reasons for diversity in religion

   d analyse and compare the evidence and arguments used when considering issues of truth in religion and philosophy

   e discuss and evaluate how religious beliefs and teachings inform answers to ultimate questions and ethical issues

   f apply a wide range of religious and philosophical vocabulary consistently and accurately, recognising both the power and limitations of language in expressing religious ideas and beliefs

   g interpret and evaluate a range of sources, texts and authorities, from a variety of contexts

   h interpret a variety of forms of religious and spiritual expression.

Learning from religion

2 Pupils should be taught to:

   a reflect on the relationship between beliefs, teachings and ultimate questions, communicating their own ideas and using reasoned arguments

   b evaluate the challenges and tensions of belonging to a religion and the impact of religion in the contemporary world, expressing their own ideas

   c express insights into the significance and value of religion and other world views on human relationships personally, locally and globally

   d reflect and evaluate their own and others' beliefs about world issues such as peace and conflict, wealth and poverty and the importance of the environment, communicating their own ideas

   e express their own beliefs and ideas, using a variety of forms of expression.

Throughout key stage 3, pupils extend their understanding of Christianity and at least two of the other principal religions in a local, national and global context. They deepen their understanding of important beliefs, concepts and issues of truth and authority in religion. They apply their understanding of religious and philosophical beliefs, teachings and practices to a range of ultimate questions and ethical issues, with a focus on self-awareness, relationships, rights and responsibilities. They enquire into and explain some personal, philosophical, theological and cultural reasons for similarities and differences in religious beliefs and values, both within and between religions. They interpret religious texts and other sources, recognising both the power and limitations of language and other forms of communication in expressing ideas and beliefs. They reflect on the impact of religion and belief in the world, considering both the importance of interfaith dialogue and the tensions that exist within and between religions and beliefs. They develop their evaluative skills, showing reasoned and balanced viewpoints when considering their own and others' responses to religious, philosophical and spiritual issues.

1a → Links to other subjects
This builds on Ci1b, where pupils develop their knowledge and understanding of national, regional, religious and ethnic identities in the United Kingdom and the need for mutual respect and understanding.

1c → ICT opportunity
Pupils could use the internet to investigate the websites of a range of religious groups.

1d → Links to other subjects
This builds on En3/1i and 3m, where pupils develop logical arguments and cite evidence, and form their own views, taking into account a range of evidence and options.

1d → Attitudes
Pupils have the opportunity to develop open-mindedness.

1h → Links to other subjects
This requirement builds on A&D5d where pupils investigate art, craft and design in a variety of styles and traditions and from a range of historical, social and cultural contexts.

Breadth of study

3 During the key stage, pupils should be taught the **Knowledge, skills and understanding** through the following areas of study:

Religions and beliefs

a Christianity

b at least two other principal religions

c a religious community with a significant local presence, where appropriate

d a secular world view, where appropriate

Themes

e beliefs and concepts: the key ideas and questions of meaning in religions and beliefs, including issues related to God, truth, the world, human life, and life after death

f authority: different sources of authority and how they inform believers' lives

g religion and science: issues of truth, explanation, meaning and purpose

h expressions of spirituality: how and why human self-understanding and experiences are expressed in a variety of forms

i ethics and relationships: questions and influences that inform ethical and moral choices, including forgiveness and issues of good and evil

j rights and responsibilities: what religions and beliefs say about human rights and responsibilities, social justice and citizenship

k global issues: what religions and beliefs say about health, wealth, war, animal rights and the environment

l interfaith dialogue: a study of relationships, conflicts and collaboration within and between religions and beliefs

Experiences and opportunities

m encountering people from different religious, cultural and philosophical groups, who can express a range of convictions on religious and ethical issues

n visiting, where possible, places of major religious significance and using opportunities in ICT to enhance pupils' understanding of religion

o discussing, questioning and evaluating important issues in religion and philosophy, including ultimate questions and ethical issues

p reflecting on and carefully evaluating their own beliefs and values and those of others in response to their learning in religious education, using reasoned, balanced arguments

q using a range of forms of expression (such as art and design, music, dance, drama, writing, ICT) to communicate their ideas and responses creatively and thoughtfully

r exploring the connections between religious education and other subject areas such as the arts, humanities, literature, science.

2b → Attitudes
Pupils have the opportunity to develop respect for all.

2d → Links to other subjects
This builds on Gg5a–b and 6i–k, where pupils investigate issues concerning the environment and sustainability and the need to reflect on and evaluate their own and other beliefs about the issues.

2e → ICT opportunity
Pupils could use presentation software, digital video and desktop publishing to express their own beliefs and ideas.

3e–f → Links to other subjects
This builds on Hi7a–b, where pupils learn about significant events, people and changes from the recent and more distant past, and history from a variety of perspectives including political, religious, social, cultural and aesthetic.

3g → Links to other subjects
This builds on Sc1a–c, where pupils learn about empirical questions, evidence and scientific explanations using contemporary examples.

3i → Links to other subjects
This builds on PSHE3b–l, where pupils learn about the nature of friendship, the range of lifestyles and relationships, the role and importance of marriage in family relationships and the value of family life.

3n → ICT opportunity
Pupils could use CD-ROMs to experience a virtual visit and videoconference to develop their understanding of places of major religious significance.

Ages 14–19

Knowledge, skills and understanding

Learning about religion

1 Students should be taught to:

a investigate, study and interpret significant religious, philosophical and ethical issues, including the study of religious and spiritual experience, in light of their own sense of identity, experience and commitments

b think rigorously and present coherent, widely informed and detailed arguments about beliefs, ethics, values and issues, drawing well-substantiated conclusions

c develop their understanding of the principal methods by which religions and spirituality are studied

d draw upon, interpret and evaluate the rich and varied forms of creative expression in religious life

e use specialist vocabulary to evaluate critically both the power and limitations of religious language.

Learning from religion

2 Students should be taught to:

a reflect on, express and justify their own opinions in light of their learning about religion and their study of religious, philosophical, moral and spiritual questions

b develop their own values and attitudes in order to recognise their rights and responsibilities in light of their learning about religion

c relate their learning in religious education to the wider world, gaining a sense of personal autonomy in preparation for adult life

d develop skills that are useful in a wide range of careers and in adult life generally, especially skills of critical enquiry, creative problem-solving, and communication in a variety of media.

What should schools do?

Schools should provide religious education to every student in accordance with legal requirements.

Religious education is a statutory subject for all registered students, including students in the school sixth form, except those withdrawn by their parents. It must be made available in sixth-form colleges to students who wish to take it. Although it is not a requirement in colleges of further education, similar arrangements should apply.

Religious education must be taught according to the locally agreed syllabus or faith community guidelines, which often specify accredited courses as the programme of study in religious education at key stage 4 and post-16.

Throughout this phase, students analyse and interpret a wide range of religious, philosophical and ethical concepts in increasing depth. They investigate issues of diversity within and between religions and the ways in which religion and spirituality are expressed in philosophy, ethics, science and the arts. They expand and balance their evaluations of the impact of religions on individuals, communities and societies, locally, nationally and globally. They understand the importance of dialogue between and among different religions and beliefs. They gain a greater understanding of how religion and belief contribute to community cohesion, recognising the various perceptions people have regarding the roles of religion in the world.

1a → Links to other subjects
This builds on Sc4a–c, where students learn about scientific controversies and ethical issues.

1a → Links to other subjects
This builds on Ci1b, where students learn about the origins and implications of the diverse national, regional, religious and ethnic identities in the United Kingdom and the need for mutual respect and understanding.

1b → ICT opportunity
Students could use a wide range of presentation software to present their findings.

1d → Attitudes
Students have the opportunity to develop appreciation and wonder.

1e → Links to other subjects
This builds on En2/2a–c, where students learn about how and why texts have been influential and significant, and the appeal and importance of these texts over time.

While there is no legal requirement that students must sit public examinations, students deserve the opportunity to have their learning in the statutory curriculum subject of religious education accredited. Accreditation can be through courses leading to qualifications with the title 'Religious studies' and/or other approved courses that require the study of religion and ethics. ASCs are recommended to include a requirement that religious education should be taught at the following ages through accredited qualifications so that, from the earliest opportunity, schools provide:

- for all students aged 14–16, at least one course in religious education or religious studies leading to a qualification approved under Section 96[6]
- for all students aged 16–19, at least one course in religious education or religious studies leading to a qualification approved under Section 96 that represents progression from 14–16.

How can schools fulfil their requirement to provide religious education to all registered students?

Schools should plan for continuity of provision of religious education that is progressive and rigorous from key stage 3 for all students. Schools can make this possible by providing access to discrete courses or units leading to qualifications that meet legal requirements regarding the study of Christianity, and/or other principal religions, and/or other beliefs, world views or philosophies, within the context of a pluralistic society.

All courses should provide opportunities within and beyond school for learning that involves first-hand experiences and activities involving people, places and events (for example the local area, places of worship and community activities, public meetings, and places of employment, education, training or recreation). Students will have different experiences of religious education according to the courses chosen.

2b → Links to other subjects
This builds on PSHE3a–c, where students are taught about the power of prejudice, and to challenge racism and discrimination assertively.

2c → Attitudes
Students have the opportunity to develop self-awareness.

2d → Links to other subjects
This builds on ICT1a, 2b and 3a–b, where students analyse the information they need and ways they will use it, presenting it in forms that are sensitive to the needs of particular audiences.

---

[6] Section 96 of the Learning and Skills Act 2000. This requires maintained schools to provide only qualifications approved by the Secretary of State.

The attainment targets for religious education

About the attainment targets

The attainment targets for religious education set out the knowledge, skills and understanding that pupils of different abilities and maturities are expected to have by the end of key stages 1, 2 and 3. As with the National Curriculum subjects, the attainment targets consist of eight level descriptions of increasing difficulty, plus a description for exceptional performance above level 8. Each level description describes the types and range of performance that pupils working at that level should characteristically demonstrate. Apart from their summative use, these level descriptions can be used in assessment for learning.

The key indicators of attainment in religious education are contained in two attainment targets:

■ Attainment target 1: Learning about religion
■ Attainment target 2: Learning from religion.

Learning about religion includes enquiry into, and investigation of, the nature of religion. It focuses on beliefs, teachings and sources, practices and ways of life and forms of expression. It includes the skills of interpretation, analysis and explanation. Pupils learn to communicate their knowledge and understanding using specialist vocabulary. It includes identifying and developing an understanding of ultimate questions and ethical issues.

Learning from religion is concerned with developing pupils' reflection on, and response to, their own experiences and learning about religion. It develops pupils' skills of application, interpretation and evaluation of what they learn about religion, particularly questions of identity and belonging, meaning, purpose, truth, values and commitments, and communicating their responses.

The level descriptions provide the basis to make judgements about pupils' performance at the end of key stages 1, 2 and 3. In the foundation stage, children's attainment is assessed in relation to the early learning goals. At key stage 4, national qualifications are the main means of assessing attainment in religious education.

Range of levels within which the great majority of pupils are expected to work		Expected attainment for the majority of pupils at the end of the key stage	
Key stage 1	**1–3**	At age 7	**2**
Key stage 2	**2–5**	At age 11	**4**
Key stage 3	**3–7**	At age 14	**5/6**

Assessing attainment at the end of a key stage

The two attainment targets, **Learning about religion** and **Learning from religion** are closely related and neither should be taught in isolation. Therefore, assessment needs to take place in relation to both attainment targets.

In deciding on a pupil's level of attainment at the end of a key stage, teachers should judge which description best fits the pupil's performance. When doing so, each description should be considered alongside descriptions for adjacent levels. There are no national statutory assessment requirements in religious education, but schools must report to parents on pupils' progress in religious education. Agreed syllabuses may require schools to report progress in terms of levels of attainment.

It is important to note that not all aspects of religious education can be assessed. For example, pupils may express personal views and ideas that, although integral to teaching and learning, would not be appropriate for formal assessment.

The level descriptions for **Attainment target 1: Learning about religion** refer to how pupils develop their knowledge, skills and understanding with reference to:
- beliefs, teachings and sources
- practices and ways of life
- forms of expression.

The level descriptions for **Attainment target 2: Learning from religion** refer to how pupils, in the light of their learning about religion, express their responses and insights with regard to questions and issues about:
- identity and belonging
- meaning, purpose and truth
- values and commitments.

Attainment targets for religious education

Level 1
Attainment target 1
Pupils use some religious words and phrases to recognise and name features of religious life and practice. They can recall religious stories and recognise symbols, and other verbal and visual forms of religious expression.
Attainment target 2
Pupils talk about their own experiences and feelings, what they find interesting or puzzling and what is of value and concern to themselves and to others.

Level 2
Attainment target 1
Pupils use religious words and phrases to identify some features of religion and its importance for some people. They begin to show awareness of similarities in religions. Pupils retell religious stories and suggest meanings for religious actions and symbols. They identify how religion is expressed in different ways.
Attainment target 2
Pupils ask, and respond sensitively to, questions about their own and others' experiences and feelings. They recognise that some questions cause people to wonder and are difficult to answer. In relation to matters of right and wrong, they recognise their own values and those of others.

Level 3
Attainment target 1
Pupils use a developing religious vocabulary to describe some key features of religions, recognising similarities and differences. They make links between beliefs and sources, including religious stories and sacred texts. They begin to identify the impact religion has on believers' lives. They describe some forms of religious expression.
Attainment target 2
Pupils identify what influences them, making links between aspects of their own and others' experiences. They ask important questions about religion and beliefs, making links between their own and others' responses. They make links between values and commitments, and their own attitudes and behaviour.

Level 4
Attainment target 1
Pupils use a developing religious vocabulary to describe and show understanding of sources, practices, beliefs, ideas, feelings and experiences. They make links between them, and describe some similarities and differences both within and between religions. They describe the impact of religion on people's lives. They suggest meanings for a range of forms of religious expression.
Attainment target 2
Pupils raise, and suggest answers to, questions of identity, belonging, meaning, purpose, truth, values and commitments. They apply their ideas to their own and other people's lives. They describe what inspires and influences themselves and others.

Level 5
Attainment target 1
Pupils use an increasingly wide religious vocabulary to explain the impact of beliefs on individuals and communities. They describe why people belong to religions. They understand that similarities and differences illustrate distinctive beliefs within and between religions and suggest possible reasons for this. They explain how religious sources are used to provide answers to ultimate questions and ethical issues, recognising diversity in forms of religious, spiritual and moral expression, within and between religions.
Attainment target 2
Pupils ask, and suggest answers to, questions of identity, belonging, meaning, purpose and truth, values and commitments, relating them to their own and others' lives. They explain what inspires and influences them, expressing their own and others' views on the challenges of belonging to a religion.

Level 6

Attainment target 1

Pupils use religious and philosophical vocabulary to give informed accounts of religions and beliefs, explaining the reasons for diversity within and between them. They explain why the impact of religions and beliefs on individuals, communities and societies varies. They interpret sources and arguments, explaining the reasons that are used in different ways by different traditions to provide answers to ultimate questions and ethical issues. They interpret the significance of different forms of religious, spiritual and moral expression.

Attainment target 2

Pupils use reasoning and examples to express insights into the relationship between beliefs, teachings and world issues. They express insights into their own and others' views on questions of identity and belonging, meaning, purpose and truth. They consider the challenges of belonging to a religion in the contemporary world, focusing on values and commitments.

Level 7

Attainment target 1

Pupils use a wide religious and philosophical vocabulary to show a coherent understanding of a range of religions and beliefs. They analyse issues, values and questions of meaning and truth. They account for the influence of history and culture on aspects of religious life and practice. They explain why the consequences of belonging to a faith are not the same for all people within the same religion or tradition. They use some of the principal methods by which religion, spirituality and ethics are studied, including the use of a variety of sources, evidence and forms of expression.

Attainment target 2

Pupils articulate personal and critical responses to questions of meaning, purpose and truth and ethical issues. They evaluate the significance of religious and other views for understanding questions of human relationships, belonging, identity, society, values and commitments, using appropriate evidence and examples.

Level 8

Attainment target 1

Pupils use a comprehensive religious and philosophical vocabulary to analyse a range of religions and beliefs. They contextualise interpretations of religion with reference to historical, cultural, social and philosophical ideas. They critically evaluate the impact of religions and beliefs on differing communities and societies. They analyse differing interpretations of religious, spiritual and moral sources, using some of the principal methods by which religion, spirituality and ethics are studied. They interpret and evaluate varied forms of religious, spiritual and moral expression.

Attainment target 2

Pupils coherently analyse a wide range of viewpoints on questions of identity, belonging, meaning, purpose, truth, values and commitments. They synthesise a range of evidence, arguments, reflections and examples, fully justifying their own views and ideas and providing a detailed evaluation of the perspectives of others.

Exceptional performance

Attainment target 1

Pupils use a complex religious, moral and philosophical vocabulary to provide a consistent and detailed analysis of religions and beliefs. They evaluate in depth the importance of religious diversity in a pluralistic society. They clearly recognise the extent to which the impact of religion and beliefs on different communities and societies has changed over time. They provide a detailed analysis of how religious, spiritual and moral sources are interpreted in different ways, evaluating the principal methods by which religion and spirituality are studied. They synthesise effectively their accounts of the varied forms of religious, spiritual and moral expression.

Attainment target 2

Pupils analyse in depth a wide range of perspectives on questions of identity and belonging, meaning, purpose and truth, and values and commitments. They give independent, well-informed and highly reasoned insights into their own and others' perspectives on religious and spiritual issues, providing well-substantiated and balanced conclusions.

Appendix: General teaching requirements

Inclusion: providing effective learning opportunities for all pupils

Schools have a responsibility to provide a broad and balanced curriculum for all pupils. The National Curriculum is the starting point for planning a school curriculum that meets the specific needs of individuals and groups of pupils. This statutory inclusion statement on providing effective learning opportunities for all pupils outlines how teachers can modify, as necessary, the National Curriculum programmes of study to provide all pupils with relevant and appropriately challenging work at each key stage. It sets out three principles that are essential to developing a more inclusive curriculum:

A   Setting suitable learning challenges

B   Responding to pupils' diverse learning needs

C   Overcoming potential barriers to learning and assessment for individuals and groups of pupils.

Applying these principles should keep to a minimum the need for aspects of the National Curriculum to be disapplied for a pupil.

Schools are able to provide other curricular opportunities outside the National Curriculum to meet the needs of individuals or groups of pupils, such as speech and language therapy and mobility training.

Three principles for inclusion

In planning and teaching the National Curriculum, teachers are required to have due regard to the following principles.

A Setting suitable learning challenges

1   Teachers should aim to give every pupil the opportunity to experience success in learning and to achieve as high a standard as possible. The National Curriculum programmes of study set out what most pupils should be taught at each key stage – but teachers should teach the knowledge, skills and understanding in ways that suit their pupils' abilities. This may mean choosing knowledge, skills and understanding from earlier or later key stages so that individual pupils can make progress and show what they can achieve. Where it is appropriate for pupils to make extensive use of content from an earlier key stage, there may not be time to teach all aspects of the age-related programmes of study. A similarly flexible approach will be needed to take account of any gaps in pupils' learning resulting from missed or interrupted schooling [for example, that may be experienced by travellers, refugees, those in care or those with long-term medical conditions, including pupils with neurological problems, such as head injuries, and those with degenerative conditions].

2   For pupils whose attainments fall significantly below the expected levels at a particular key stage, a much greater degree of differentiation will be necessary. In these circumstances, teachers may need to use the content of the programmes of study as a resource or to provide a context, in planning learning appropriate to the age and requirements of their pupils.

3   For pupils whose attainments significantly exceed the expected level of attainment within one or more subjects during a particular key stage, teachers will need to plan suitably challenging work. As well as drawing on materials from later key stages or higher levels of study, teachers may plan further differentiation by extending the breadth and depth of study within individual subjects or by planning work which draws on the content of different subjects.

B   Responding to pupils' diverse learning needs

1   When planning, teachers should set high expectations and provide opportunities for all pupils to achieve, including boys and girls, pupils with special educational needs, pupils with disabilities, pupils from all social and cultural backgrounds, pupils of different ethnic groups including travellers, refugees and asylum seekers, and those from diverse linguistic backgrounds. Teachers need to be aware that pupils bring to school different experiences, interests and strengths which will influence the way in which they learn. Teachers should plan their approaches to teaching and learning so that all pupils can take part in lessons fully and effectively.

2   To ensure that they meet the full range of pupils' needs, teachers should be aware of the requirements of the equal opportunities legislation that covers race, gender and disability.

3   Teachers should take specific action to respond to pupils' diverse needs by:
   a   creating effective learning environments
   b   securing their motivation and concentration
   c   providing equality of opportunity through teaching approaches
   d   using appropriate assessment approaches
   e   setting targets for learning.

Examples for B/3a – creating effective learning environments
Teachers create effective learning environments in which:

- the contribution of all pupils is valued
- all pupils can feel secure and are able to contribute appropriately
- stereotypical views are challenged and pupils learn to appreciate and view positively differences in others, whether arising from race, gender, ability or disability
- pupils learn to take responsibility for their actions and behaviours both in school and in the wider community
- all forms of bullying and harassment, including racial harassment, are challenged
- pupils are enabled to participate safely in clothing appropriate to their religious beliefs, particularly in subjects such as science, design and technology and physical education.

Examples for B/3b – securing motivation and concentration

Teachers secure pupils' motivation and concentration by:

- using teaching approaches appropriate to different learning styles
- using, where appropriate, a range of organisational approaches, such as setting, grouping or individual work, to ensure that learning needs are properly addressed
- varying subject content and presentation so that this matches their learning needs
- planning work which builds on their interests and cultural experiences
- planning appropriately challenging work for those whose ability and understanding are in advance of their language skills
- using materials which reflect social and cultural diversity and provide positive images of race, gender and disability
- planning and monitoring the pace of work so that they all have a chance to learn effectively and achieve success
- taking action to maintain interest and continuity of learning for pupils who may be absent for extended periods of time.

Examples for B/3c – providing equality of opportunity

Teaching approaches that provide equality of opportunity include:

- ensuring that boys and girls are able to participate in the same curriculum, particularly in science, design and technology and physical education
- taking account of the interests and concerns of boys and girls by using a range of activities and contexts for work and allowing a variety of interpretations and outcomes, particularly in English, science, design and technology, ICT, art and design, music and physical education
- avoiding gender stereotyping when organising pupils into groups, assigning them to activities or arranging access to equipment, particularly in science, design and technology, ICT, music and physical education
- taking account of pupils' specific religious or cultural beliefs relating to the representation of ideas or experiences or to the use of particular types of equipment, particularly in science, design and technology, ICT and art and design
- enabling the fullest possible participation of pupils with disabilities or particular medical needs in all subjects, offering positive role models and making provision, where necessary, to facilitate access to activities with appropriate support, aids or adaptations. (See **Overcoming potential barriers to learning and assessment for individuals and groups of pupils.**)

Examples for B/3d – using appropriate assessment approaches

Teachers use appropriate assessment approaches that:

- allow for different learning styles and ensure that pupils are given the chance and encouragement to demonstrate their competence and attainment through appropriate means
- are familiar to the pupils and for which they have been adequately prepared
- use materials which are free from discrimination and stereotyping in any form
- provide clear and unambiguous feedback to pupils to aid further learning.

Examples for B/3e – setting targets for learning

Teachers set targets for learning that:

- build on pupils' knowledge, experiences, interests and strengths to improve areas of weakness and demonstrate progression over time
- are attainable and yet challenging and help pupils to develop their self-esteem and confidence in their ability to learn.

C Overcoming potential barriers to learning and assessment for individuals and groups of pupils

A minority of pupils will have particular learning and assessment requirements which go beyond the provisions described in sections A and B and, if not addressed, could create barriers to learning. These requirements are likely to arise as a consequence of a pupil having a special educational need or disability or may be linked to a pupil's progress in learning English as an additional language.

1 Teachers must take account of these requirements and make provision, where necessary, to support individuals or groups of pupils to enable them to participate effectively in the curriculum and assessment activities. During end of key stage assessments, teachers should bear in mind that special arrangements are available to support individual pupils.

Pupils with special educational needs

2 Curriculum planning and assessment for pupils with special educational needs must take account of the type and extent of the difficulty experienced by the pupil. Teachers will encounter a wide range of pupils with special educational needs, some of whom will also have disabilities (see paragraphs C/4 and C/5). In many cases, the action necessary to respond to an individual's requirements for curriculum access will be met through greater differentiation of tasks and materials, consistent with school-based intervention as set out in the SEN Code of Practice. A smaller number of pupils may need access to specialist equipment and approaches or to alternative or adapted activities, consistent with school-based intervention augmented by advice and support from external specialists as described in the SEN Code of Practice, or, in exceptional circumstances, with a statement of special educational need. Teachers should, where appropriate, work closely with representatives of other agencies who may be supporting the pupil.

3 Teachers should take specific action to provide access to learning for pupils with special educational needs by:
  a providing for pupils who need help with communication, language and literacy
  b planning, where necessary, to develop pupils' understanding through the use of all available senses and experiences
  c planning for pupils' full participation in learning and in physical and practical activities
  d helping pupils to manage their behaviour, to take part in learning effectively and safely and, at key stage 4, to prepare for work
  e helping individuals to manage their emotions, particularly trauma or stress, and to take part in learning.

Examples for C/3a – helping with communication, language and literacy

Teachers provide for pupils who need help with communication, language and literacy through:

- using texts that pupils can read and understand
- using visual and written materials in different formats, including large print, symbol text and braille
- using ICT, other technological aids and taped materials
- using alternative and augmentative communication, including signs and symbols
- using translators, communicators and amanuenses.

Examples for C/3b – developing understanding

Teachers develop pupils' understanding through the use of all available senses and experiences, by:

- using materials and resources that pupils can access through sight, touch, sound, taste or smell
- using word descriptions and other stimuli to make up for a lack of first-hand experiences
- using ICT, visual and other materials to increase pupils' knowledge of the wider world
- encouraging pupils to take part in everyday activities such as play, drama, class visits and exploring the environment.

Examples for C/3c – planning for full participation

Teachers plan for pupils' full participation in learning and in physical and practical activities through:

- using specialist aids and equipment
- providing support from adults or peers when needed
- adapting tasks or environments
- providing alternative activities, where necessary.

Examples for C/3d – managing behaviour

Teachers help pupils to manage their behaviour, take part in learning effectively and safely and, at key stage 4, prepare for work by:

- setting realistic demands and stating them explicitly
- using positive behaviour management, including a clear structure of rewards and sanctions
- giving pupils every chance and encouragement to develop the skills they need to work well with a partner or a group
- teaching pupils to value and respect the contribution of others
- encouraging and teaching independent working skills
- teaching essential safety rules.

Examples for C/3e – managing emotions

Teachers help individuals manage their emotions and take part
in learning through:

- identifying aspects of learning in which the pupil will engage and
  plan short-term, easily achievable goals in selected activities
- providing positive feedback to reinforce and encourage learning and
  build self-esteem
- selecting tasks and materials sensitively to avoid unnecessary stress
  for the pupil
- creating a supportive learning environment in which the pupil feels
  safe and is able to engage with learning
- allowing time for the pupil to engage with learning and gradually
  increasing the range of activities and demands.

Pupils with disabilities

4   Not all pupils with disabilities will necessarily have special educational needs.
    Many pupils with disabilities learn alongside their peers with little need for
    additional resources beyond the aids which they use as part of their daily life,
    such as a wheelchair, a hearing aid or equipment to aid vision. Teachers must
    take action, however, in their planning to ensure that these pupils are enabled
    to participate as fully and effectively as possible within the National Curriculum
    and the statutory assessment arrangements. Potential areas of difficulty
    should be identified and addressed at the outset of work, without recourse
    to the formal provisions for disapplication.

5   Teachers should take specific action to enable the effective participation
    of pupils with disabilities by:
    a   planning appropriate amounts of time to allow for the satisfactory
        completion of tasks
    b   planning opportunities, where necessary, for the development of skills
        in practical aspects of the curriculum
    c   identifying aspects of programmes of study and attainment targets
        that may present specific difficulties for individuals.

Examples for C/5a – planning to complete tasks

Teachers plan appropriate amounts of time to allow pupils to complete tasks
satisfactorily through:

- taking account of the very slow pace at which some pupils will be able to
  record work, either manually or with specialist equipment, and of the physical
  effort required
- being aware of the high levels of concentration necessary for some pupils
  when following or interpreting text or graphics, particularly when using vision
  aids or tactile methods, and of the tiredness which may result
- allocating sufficient time, opportunity and access to equipment for pupils
  to gain information through experimental work and detailed observation,
  including the use of microscopes
- being aware of the effort required by some pupils to follow oral work, whether
  through use of residual hearing, lip reading or a signer, and of the tiredness
  or loss of concentration which may occur.

Examples for C/5b – developing skills in practical aspects

Teachers create opportunities for the development of skills in practical aspects of the curriculum through:

- providing adapted, modified or alternative activities or approaches to learning in physical education and ensuring that these have integrity and equivalence to the National Curriculum and enable pupils to make appropriate progress
- providing alternative or adapted activities in science, art and design and design and technology for pupils who are unable to manipulate tools, equipment or materials or who may be allergic to certain types of materials
- ensuring that all pupils can be included and participate safely in geography fieldwork, local studies and visits to museums, historic buildings and sites.

Examples for C/5c – overcoming specific difficulties

Teachers overcome specific difficulties for individuals presented by aspects of the programmes of study and attainment targets through:

- using approaches to enable hearing impaired pupils to learn about sound in science and music
- helping visually impaired pupils to learn about light in science, to access maps and visual resources in geography and to evaluate different products in design and technology and images in art and design
- providing opportunities for pupils to develop strength in depth where they cannot meet the particular requirements of a subject, such as the visual requirements in art and design and the singing requirements in music
- discounting these aspects in appropriate individual cases when required to make a judgement against level descriptions.

Pupils who are learning English as an additional language

6   Pupils for whom English is an additional language have diverse needs in terms of support necessary in English language learning. Planning should take account of such factors as the pupil's age, length of time in this country, previous educational experience and skills in other languages. Careful monitoring of each pupil's progress in the acquisition of English language skills and of subject knowledge and understanding will be necessary to confirm that no learning difficulties are present.

7   The ability of pupils for whom English is an additional language to take part in the National Curriculum may be ahead of their communication skills in English. Teachers should plan learning opportunities to help pupils develop their English and should aim to provide the support pupils need to take part in all subject areas.

8   Teachers should take specific action to help pupils who are learning English as an additional language by:

   a   developing their spoken and written English
   b   ensuring access to the curriculum and to assessment.

Examples for C/8a – developing spoken and written English

Teachers develop pupils' spoken and written English through:

- ensuring that vocabulary work covers both the technical and everyday meaning of key words, metaphors and idioms
- explaining clearly how speaking and writing in English are structured to achieve different purposes, across a range of subjects
- providing a variety of reading material [for example, pupils' own work, the media, ICT, literature, reference books] that highlight the different ways English is used, especially those that help pupils to understand society and culture
- ensuring that there are effective opportunities for talk and that talk is used to support writing in all subjects
- where appropriate, encouraging pupils to transfer their knowledge, skills and understanding of one language to another, pointing out similarities and differences between languages
- building on pupils' experiences of language at home and in the wider community, so that their developing uses of English and other languages support one another.

Examples for C/8b – ensuring access

Teachers make sure pupils have access to the curriculum and to assessment through:

- using accessible texts and materials that suit pupils' ages and levels of learning
- providing support by using ICT or video or audio materials, dictionaries and translators, readers and amanuenses
- using home or first language, where appropriate.

Use of language across the curriculum

1   Pupils should be taught in all subjects to express themselves correctly and appropriately and to read accurately and with understanding. Since standard English, spoken and written, is the predominant language in which knowledge and skills are taught and learned, pupils should be taught to recognise and use standard English.

Writing

2   In writing, pupils should be taught to use correct spelling and punctuation and follow grammatical conventions. They should also be taught to organise their writing in logical and coherent forms.

Speaking

3   In speaking, pupils should be taught to use language precisely and cogently.

Listening

4   Pupils should be taught to listen to others, and to respond and build on their ideas and views constructively.

Reading

5   In reading, pupils should be taught strategies to help them read with understanding, to locate and use information, to follow a process or argument and summarise, and to synthesise and adapt what they learn from their reading.

6   Pupils should be taught the technical and specialist vocabulary of subjects and how to use and spell these words. They should also be taught to use the patterns of language vital to understanding and expression in different subjects. These include the construction of sentences, paragraphs and texts that are often used in a subject [for example, language to express causality, chronology, logic, exploration, hypothesis, comparison, and how to ask questions and develop arguments].

Use of information and communication technology across the curriculum

1   Pupils should be given opportunities to apply and develop their ICT capability through the use of ICT tools to support their learning in all subjects.

2   Pupils should be given opportunities to support their work by being taught to:
    a   find things out from a variety of sources, selecting and synthesising the information to meet their needs and developing an ability to question its accuracy, bias and plausibility
    b   develop their ideas using ICT tools to amend and refine their work and enhance its quality and accuracy
    c   exchange and share information, both directly and through electronic media
    d   review, modify and evaluate their work, reflecting critically on its quality, as it progresses.